Keep Calm!

Written by John Parsons
Illustrated by Lloyd Foye

Contents	Page
Chapter 1. *Evacuate!*	4
Chapter 2. *An action-packed night*	8
Chapter 3. *Things get worse*	12
Chapter 4. *And worse!*	16
Chapter 5. *The authorities arrive*	22
Chapter 6. *The insecticide*	26
Chapter 7. *Back to normal?*	29
Verse	32

Rigby

Keep Calm!

With these characters ...

Mom and Mark

Me

The Authorities

The Doctor

"It

Setting the scene ...

I like reading scary stories—especially when I'm safely tucked in bed, and I know that nothing will happen to me! There I was, with my flashlight under the blankets, reading a great scary book. Suddenly, there were sirens approaching and lights flashing and something very strange going on outside our house. Hey, wait a minute! Aren't these scary horror stories only supposed to happen in books? They're not real, are they?

was time to panic."

Chapter 1.

Saturday was just a normal night. Mom had insisted that I clean my room again (even though I'd only done it a couple of weeks ago!). I'd finished most of my homework, and I had fed the chickens that we have out in the backyard.

    I had wanted a dog or a cat, but Mom and my stepfather, Mark, had their minds made up. No dogs, because they dig holes. No cats, because Mark is allergic to them. They said that chickens were more useful. It was the idea of collecting fresh eggs from the hens every day that convinced them.

After dinner, I was having a long, warm shower—until Mom told me to hurry up and stop wasting water! I leaped into bed. The lights were out, but I had my secret flashlight under the blankets. I was reading the scariest chapter of a really good horror story.

Just then I got the fright of my life—and it wasn't my book! A disaster was about to happen.

Our first warning of the disaster was the sound of sirens coming closer and closer. I peeked out from under the blankets. I saw the eerie flashes of blue and red lights swirling outside my bedroom window. Then I heard the urgent knocking at our front door. I felt frightened. I couldn't move.

At first, I thought it was a bit silly to call the police just because I'd been reading when I should have been asleep. Then I realized that there were ambulance sirens, too. I wasn't going to stay alone any longer. I leaped out of bed and flung open my door.

"What is it, Mom?" I yelled urgently.

"We all need to get dressed very quickly," said Mom calmly. "We have to evacuate our house."

"Speak English, Mom," I said. "What's *evacuate*?"

"We need to leave immediately," she replied calmly.

Chapter 2.

Whenever Mom speaks calmly, you know there's something *really* wrong. I was about to ask why we had to leave our house, when the answer came swirling down the hallway. It was thick, pungent, and horrible-smelling. There had been a chemical spill at the factory near our house.

Wrapped up in thick, wool blankets, Mom, Mark, and I stood on the front porch looking at all the action. Our normally quiet street had police cars, ambulances, and fire engines parked everywhere.

People in strange white overalls and breathing masks were racing into the factory at the corner of the street. Our neighbors were being bundled into ambulances. Then a paramedic came up to us and drove us away to the hospital, too.

Normally, I like a bit of excitement, but all this action in the middle of the night was a little too exciting for me. What was going to happen next? Were we going to get shots? Were we going to get horrible-tasting medicine? What would they do to us at the hospital?

After a medical checkup, we all sat in a waiting room. The nurses made us feel much calmer. They gave us cups of hot chocolate and graham crackers. No shots! No medicine! The nurses asked us to wait for the doctor. The doctor would have an explanation for what had happened.

After what seemed like ages, a very important-looking doctor came and spoke to us all.

"Good news. There's really nothing to worry about," she said. "The factory had been making some experimental insecticide. It bubbled over the sides of the huge tanks unexpectedly. We've checked and cleaned up everything in the factory. The smells have gone and there is no danger to people or pets. Thank you for your cooperation."

Thankfully, we were all allowed to go home. It was a bit of an anticlimax. The ambulance dropped us off outside our front door, and we all trudged inside.

"Let's go to bed," said Mark. "I think we've all had enough excitement for the night. I'm exhausted."

Nobody wanted to argue with that. I flopped into bed, and looked at my horror-story book, lying where I'd left it. I decided against reading any more. I didn't need any more horrors, and I was looking forward to a nice, normal sleep-in on Sunday morning.

Somehow, it didn't work out that way.

Chapter 3.

When I woke up the next morning, the sun was shining through my curtains. I must have slept in, because there was a noisy lawn-mower sound buzzing away somewhere. That was strange. No one around here mows their lawns on Sunday morning.

Just as I was about to throw off the blankets and wander on down to the kitchen, something heavy thumped onto my bed. My first thought was that it was a cat leaping onto the blankets—but then I remembered Mark's allergy to cats. Why he wasn't allergic to something useful, like vegetables, I don't know. But whatever it was, it couldn't be a *cat* in our house.

I realized that the lawn mower had stopped. I slowly peeked out from under the blankets. Feeling shocked and scared, I pulled them up again very quickly when I saw what had dropped onto my bed!

"No, Melissa," I said to myself. "You must be dreaming." I slowly peeked over the blanket again. And there it was. Staring at me, with huge round eyes. It was as big as a cat. It was black and furry like a cat. But cats don't have wings. And this six-legged creature, with wings as wide as my bed, was no cat. It was a monstrous fly!

Don't believe me? Well, take a look at this . . .

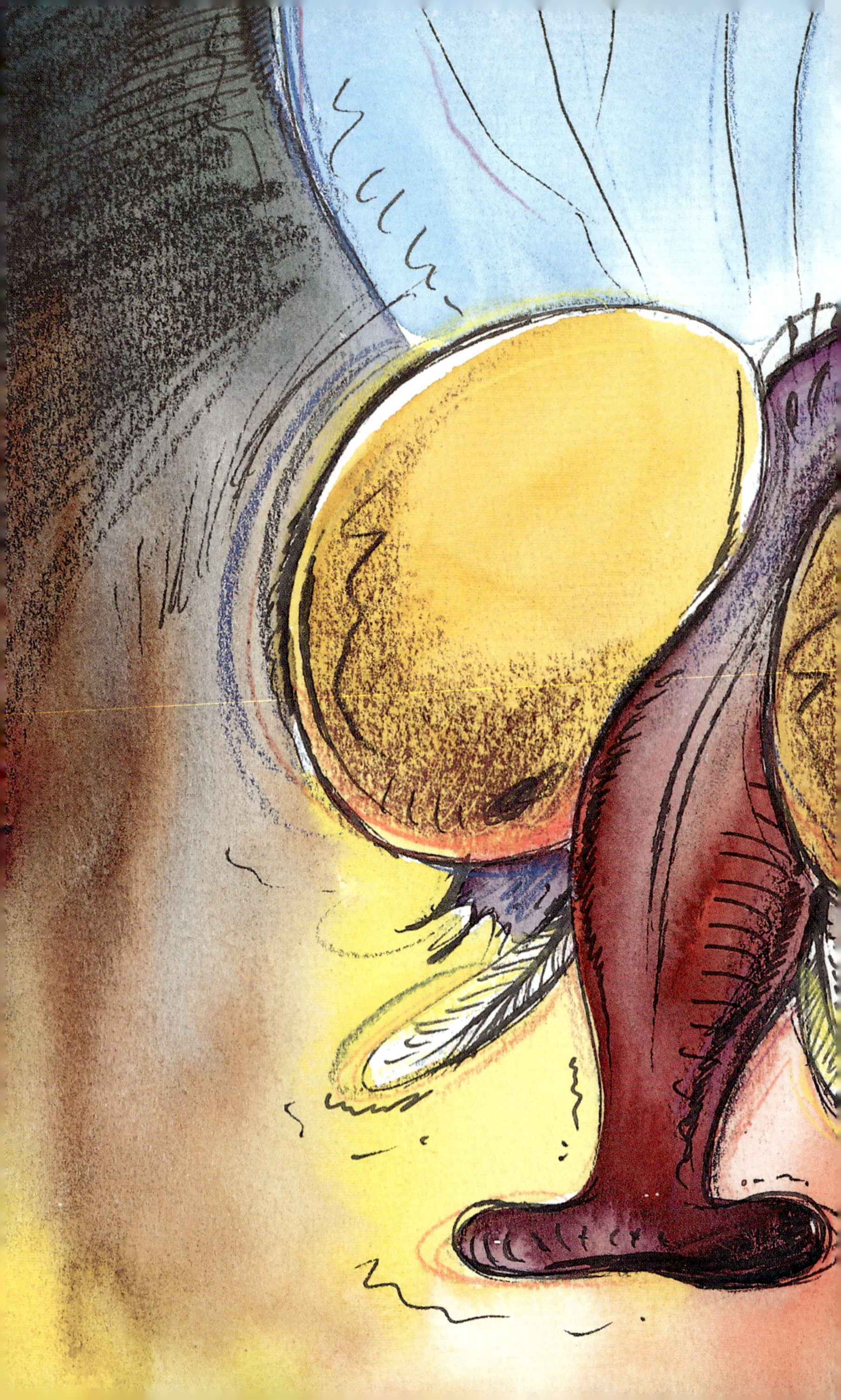

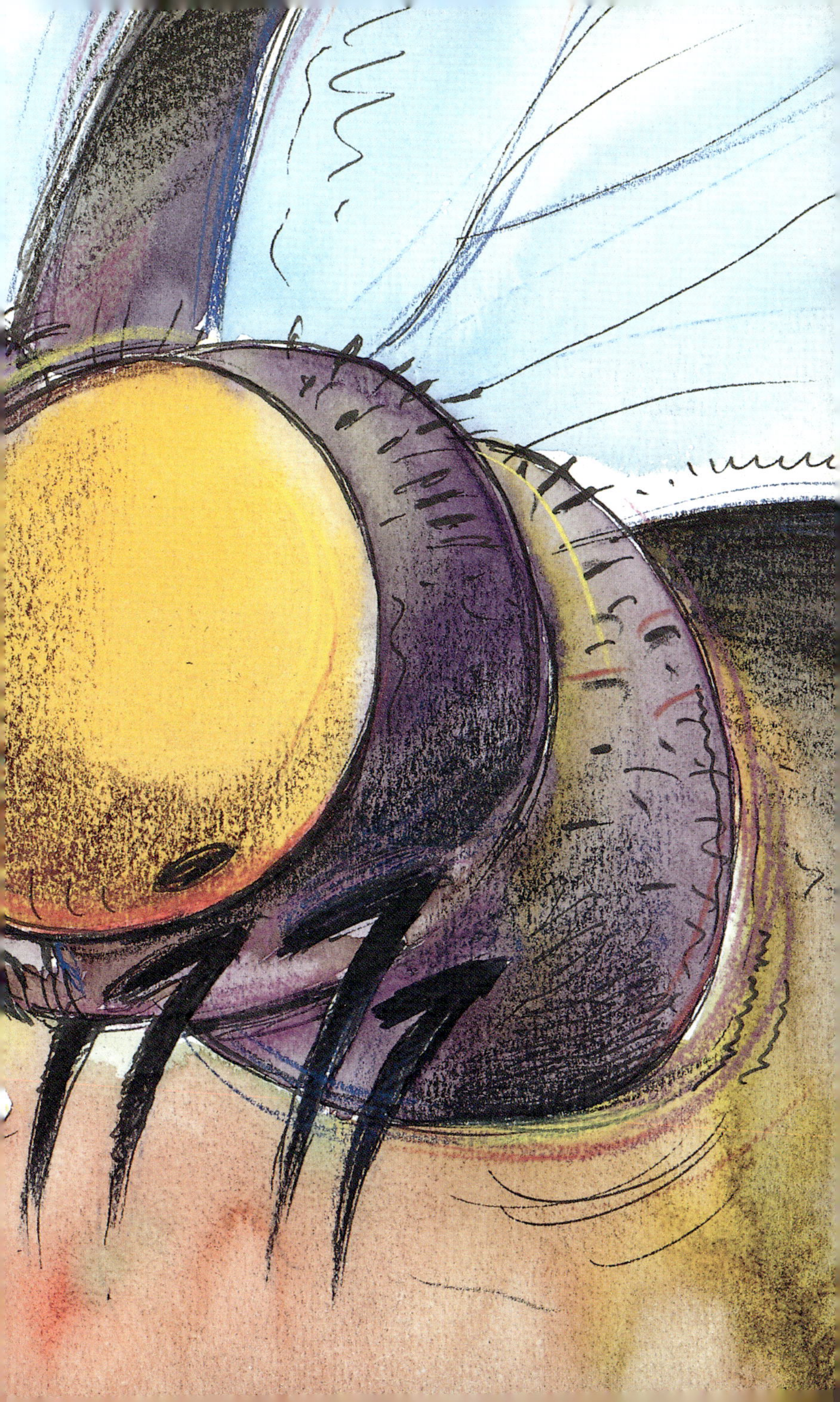

Chapter 4.

"Mom! Mark!" I screamed. "Help me!"

The gigantic fly swooped off the bed and I realized that I hadn't heard a lawn mower. It was the fly. I ducked down as it buzzed around me. The crazy fly crashed into the wall and fell on my pillow. It shook and buzzed wildly toward the other end of my room. I looked around frantically for something to defend myself with.

I was glad that I hadn't cleaned my room very well, when I spotted my tennis racket poking out from under the bed. Quickly, I reached down, grabbed it, and leaped out of bed, swatting madly at the fly. The fly buzzed even louder and zoomed around the lamp shade, rattling the lightbulbs. It circled around to face me. It had a nasty look in its eyes! It was heading straight for me!

My eyes were nearly popping out of my head as I took a huge swing at the fly.

SPLAT!

What a great shot! I wiped the greeny-yellow goo off my face. On the floor, the fly's legs were curling up. After a few wild, upside-down buzzes, it stopped moving. I sat on the edge of the bed and tried not to burst into tears. My heart was pounding, and I was shaking all over. Mom and Mark raced into my room a few seconds later and stared at the remains of the battle.

"Don't panic, dear," said Mom calmly. Mom was *calm*? I knew what that meant. It was time to panic!

Mark phoned just about everyone, from the hospital to the zoo, while Mom and I sat in the kitchen. We were desperately trying to work out why we had a monstrous, dead fly lying in my bedroom. It was not the usual problem you have to face on a sunny Sunday morning.

"The authorities are on their way," said Mark, when he had finished talking on the phone. I didn't know who the "authorities" were, but I hoped they had enormous cans of fly spray with them . . . just in case!

Just then, I had a scary thought.

"Mom," I said. "You don't think that giant fly has anything to do with the insecticide spill last night, do you?"

Before she could answer, Mark let out a huge yell and pointed at the kitchen window. Mom and I stared out the window. Ants *as big as sheep* stared back at us.

Don't believe me? Well, take a look at these . . .

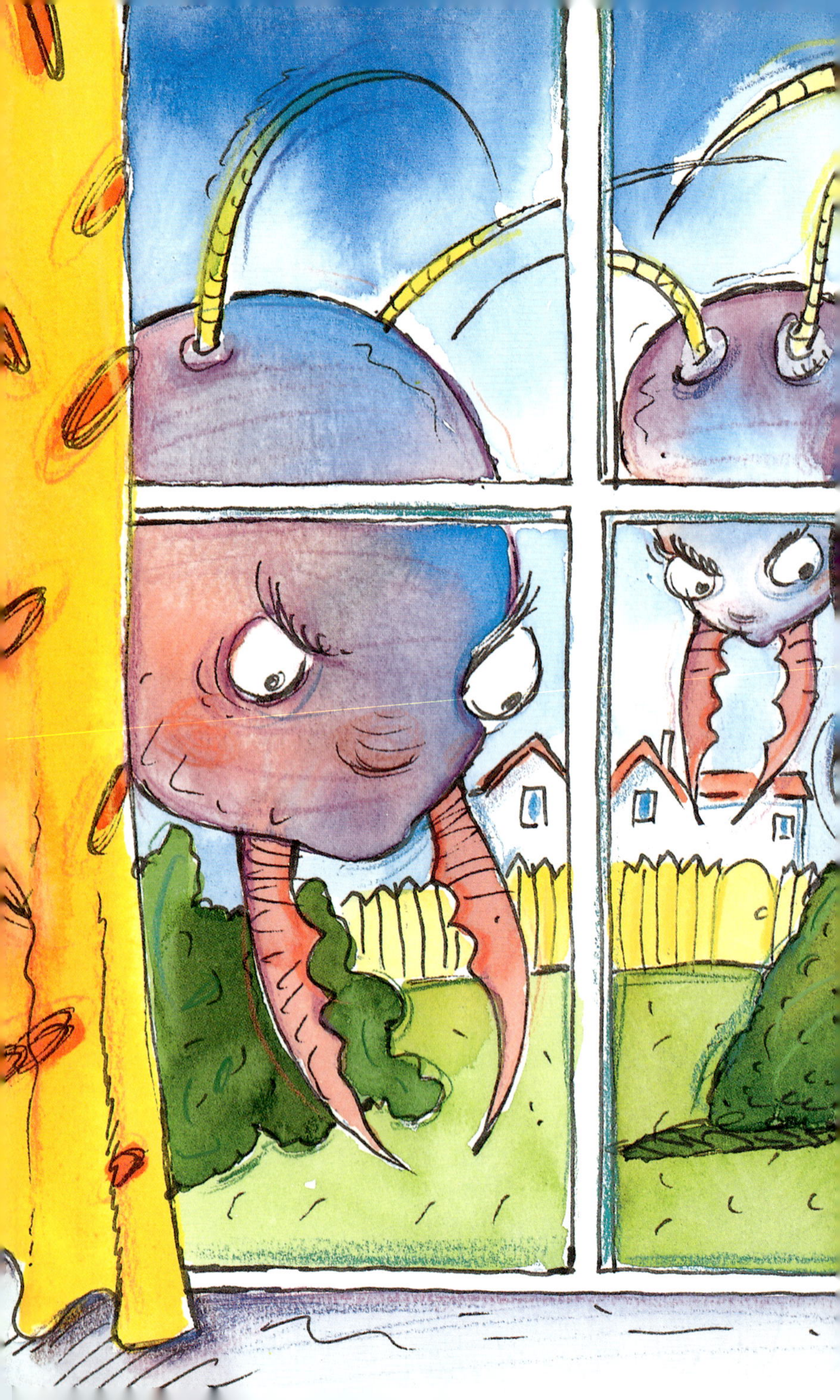

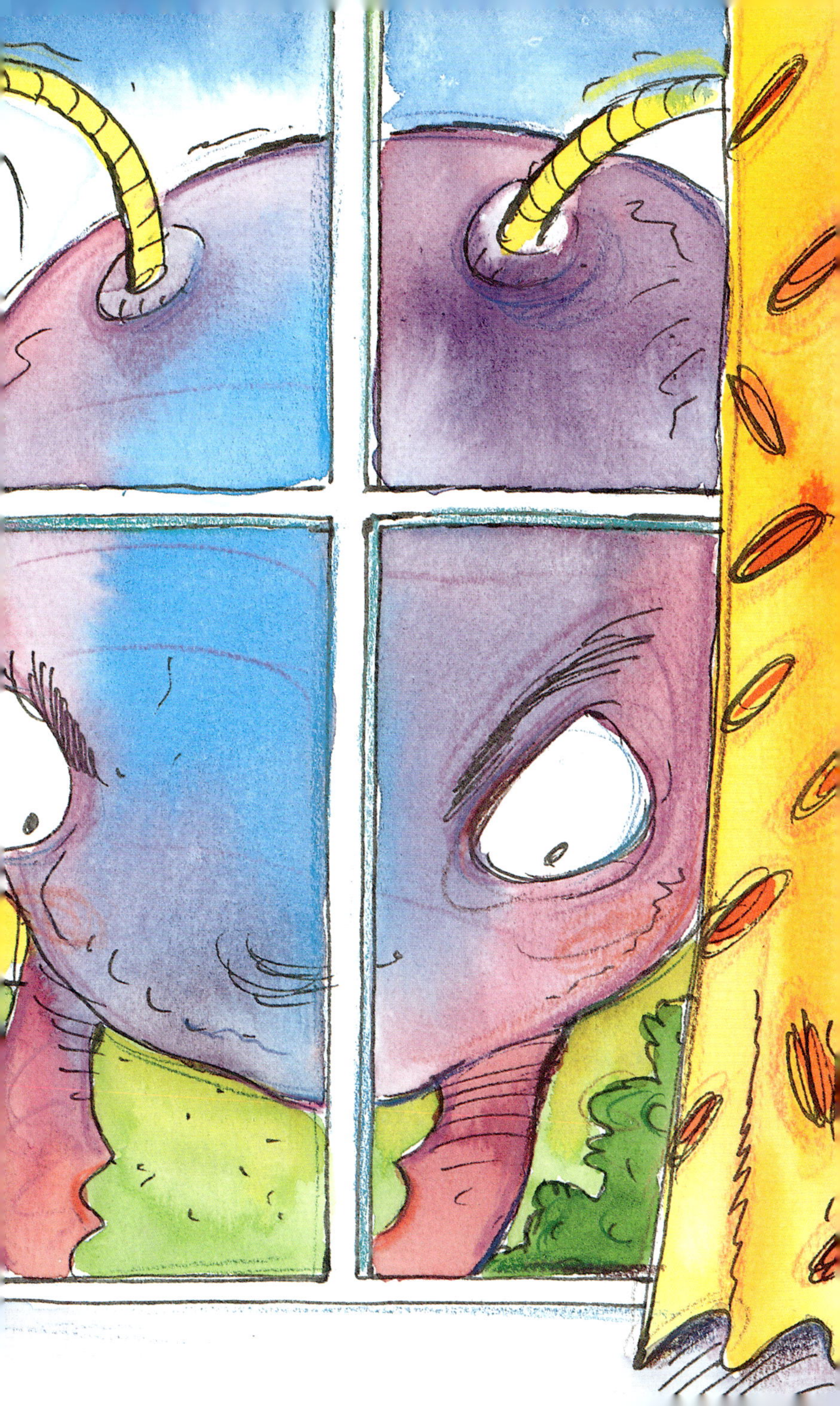

Chapter 5.

"I think I had better put the honey in the refrigerator," said Mom calmly. You could always count on Mom to be sensible in these kinds of situations.

But before she could move, our lawn started to bulge and buckle, as if it was a green pond. A gargantuan worm burst up from the ground and started to slither under the bushes. Normally, the chickens would have loved a worm meal that size. But I guessed that they were probably keeping very quiet inside the chicken coop by now. An angry ten-foot worm does *not* make a good breakfast!

By the time the "authorities" arrived, we had seen snails the size of dogs munching on the wooden fence. We had seen spiders the size of umbrellas weaving webs thicker than our clothesline, and moths the size of bats hurtling past the window. Or maybe they *were* bats. I'm sure you can understand why we didn't take a closer look!

Don't believe me? Well, take a look at these . . .

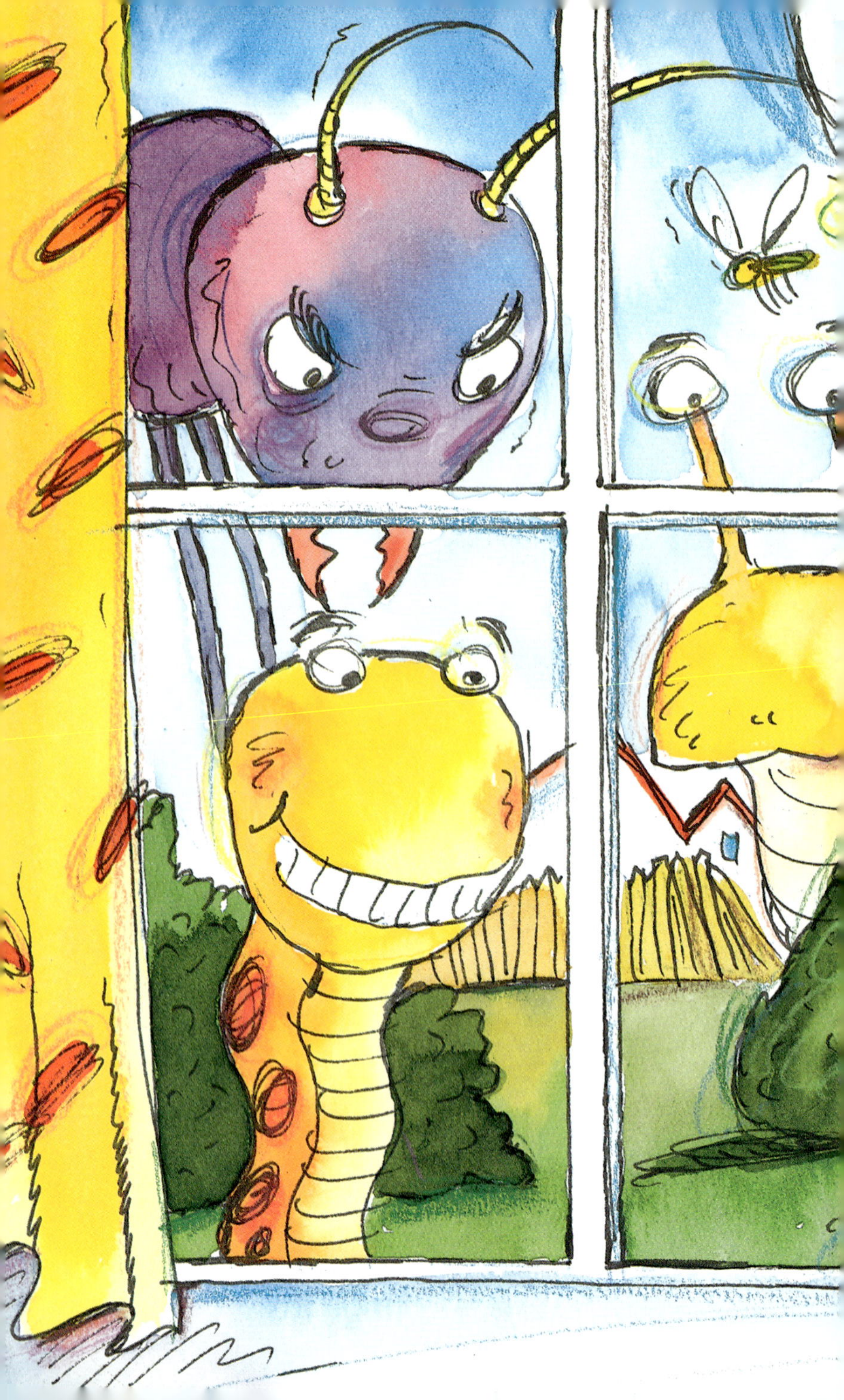

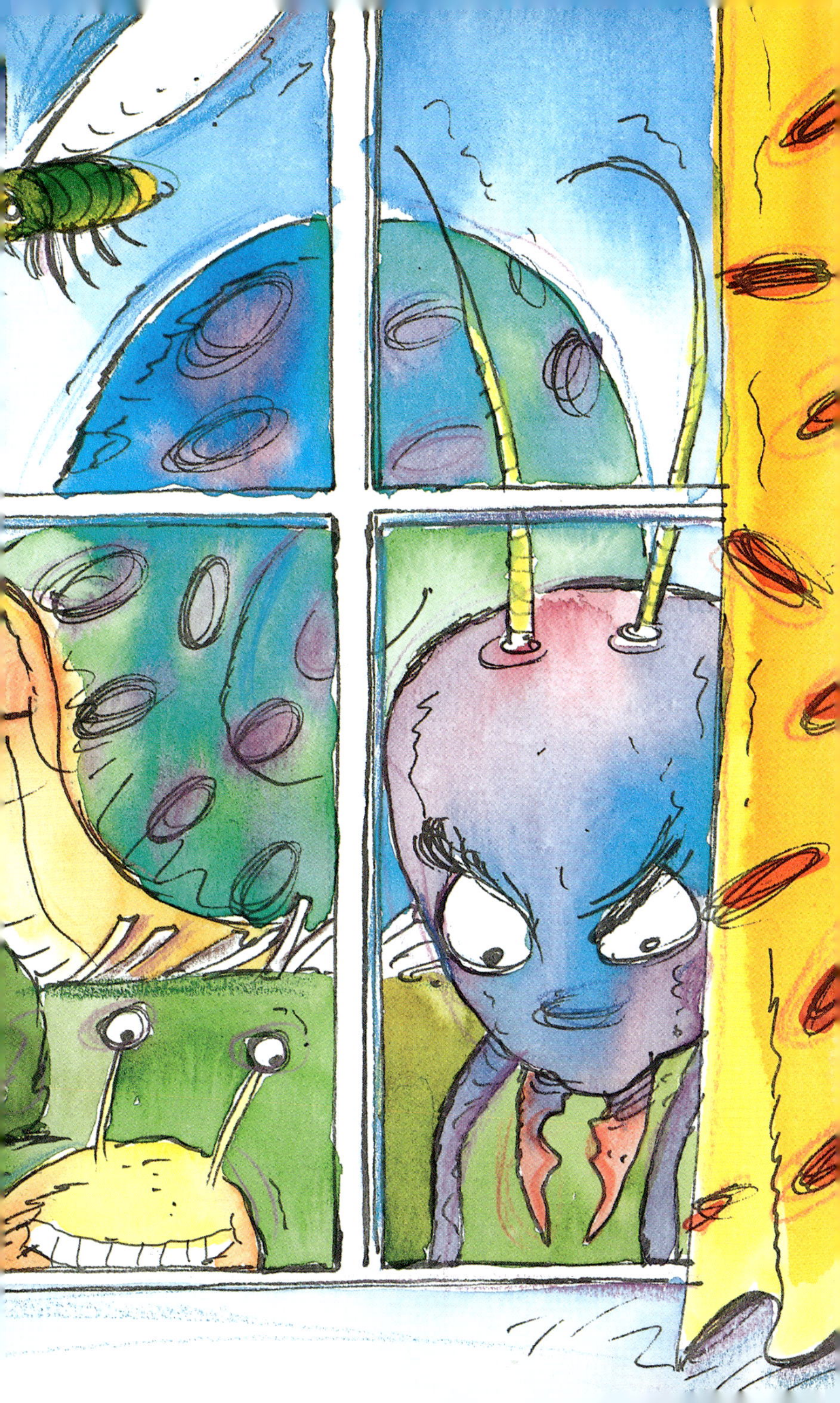

Chapter 6.

I found out that the "authorities" were the people dressed in the strange white overalls I'd seen last night. At first, I thought they'd come to take Mark away for telling such wild stories over the phone. Fortunately, they were more interested in the fact that our backyard had turned into a monster wildlife park overnight.

They raced outside and started wrestling the monstrous wildlife into cages. As they caught the last of the huge animals, we all breathed a sigh of relief. I was surprised to see the doctor from last night there, too. It seemed that she didn't work at the hospital at all, but worked for the chemical factory.

"We've been working on a special insecticide that speeds up the life cycles of small animals such as insects, spiders, and other arthropods," she explained. I made a mental note to look up "arthropods" in my dictionary later.

"Normally, a life cycle may take weeks or months to complete," she continued. "But with this new chemical, everything speeds up. We intended it to speed up their life cycles so quickly that they would only live for a day, instead of weeks. But it seems we also sped up the rate at which they grow during that life cycle."

Mom, Mark, and I pretended that we understood, and we nodded our heads.

"Anyway, none of your garden pests will live much longer than this afternoon, so those that we don't catch will just disappear by the evening. Nothing to worry about," she added, smiling.

After the authorities had slammed the van door shut on their captives, they and the doctor zoomed off down the street. Mom and Mark collapsed on the couch and just stared up at the ceiling. I went into my bedroom and threw away the horror-story book. It was extremely boring next to what we had just experienced in real life.

Chapter 7.

Happily, that night was as normal a night as we could expect after spending the day watching enormous mutant garden creatures taking over our backyard.

I showered and hopped into bed. Before I knew it, I fell asleep, and the next thing I realized, it was morning. I listened carefully. The lawn mowers sounded like lawn mowers. There was nothing on my bed. Great!

I threw off the blankets and was about to walk down to the kitchen when the window rattled and I heard a crash! I stood still. The glass rattled again. Something was banging on my window!

When I finally had enough courage to look outside, I cautiously peeked through the curtains. A huge, round, beady black eye stared back at me.

"Mom. Mark," I said very calmly. "I think we need to call the authorities again. And while we're waiting, I'll make breakfast."

"Anyone for scrambled eggs this morning? A lot of scrambled eggs!"

Can't guess what happened? Well, take a look at this . . .

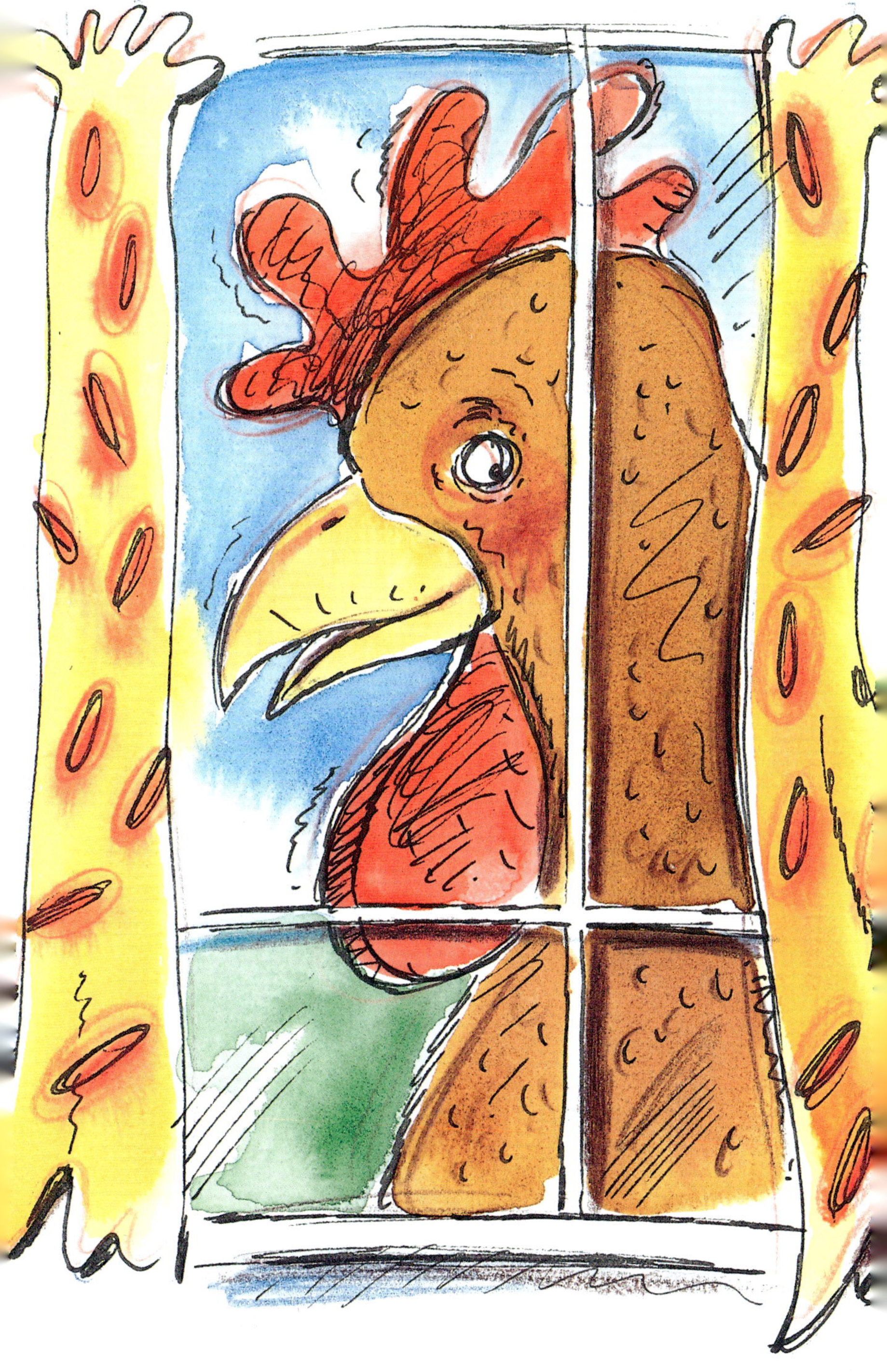

"It was time to panic."

They came crawling and slithering over the hill,
The freaky results of a chemical spill.

Doctors and scientists gave the all-clear,
"Don't worry," they said, "There's nothing to fear."

"Don't worry?" I thought. But there's nowhere to hide,
From these creatures of crazy insecticide!